Judy,

Know that you
will always have my
love, support + prayers.
Your strong faith and
Spirit inspire me.
You are stronger than you
know. God loves you + He will
get us you always.

A gift for:

My Dear Wonderful
Sister, Judy
_____

From:

Ruthann,
Sister & Godmother
_____

What Cancer Cannot Do
Copyright © 2006 by The Zondervan Corporation
ISBN-10: 0-310-81184-8
ISBN-13: 978-1-310-81184-6

Requests for information should be addressed to:
Inspirio, the gift group of Zondervan
Grand Rapids, Michigan 49530
www.inspiriogifts.com

Compiler: Phyllis Ten Elshof
Product Manager: Tom Dean
Design Manager: Michael J. Williams
Cover Design: Gayle Raymer
Interior Design: Gayle Raymer and Robin Black
Cover image: Getty Images/Amana Images/Doable

Printed in China

06 07 08 / 5 4 3 2 1

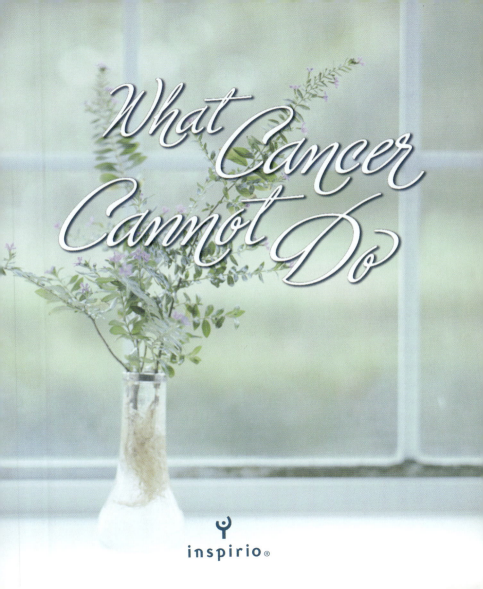

What Cancer Cannot Do

inspirio®

CONTENTS

CANCER IS SO LIMITED

It cannot cripple God's love

ETERNAL LOVE

*N*othing — not the probing fingers, the painful needle stabs, the interminable waiting for results, the surgery, the pathology reports, the naming of the dreaded word *cancer* — can separate us from the love of God.

For God made us, forming us in our mother's womb, knowing every part of us down to the very DNA of our cells. Yes, he knew that some of those cells would go astray, fleeing the intent for which they were created and following after their own way. He knew those aberrant cells were multiplying in us long before we sensed them.

But just as, in love, God brought us to salvation through the cleansing blood of his son, Jesus

Christ, so he will, in love, save us from the truly crippling effects of cancer. For when we are most afraid, his love calms us; when we feel abandoned, he surrounds us with his presence; when we feel we have lost our way, he lights up the darkness; when we are restless with pain, he soothes us with his touch; when we lose heart, thinking we will never be well again, he restores our soul.

He does this through songs in the night and Scriptures by day; through the private prayers of friends and the corporate intercession of the church; through the expert care of doctors and the compassionate hands of nurses; through the testimony of cancer survivors and the shining leadership of saints who die in the Lord. But most of all, he does this through his ever-vigilant, wholly sufficient, eternally satisfying love.

CANCER CANNOT CRIPPLE GOD'S LOVE. He loved us from the beginning, he loves us through disease, he loves us in and out of treatment, and he loves us to the end, where, someday, we will know no more tears, no more sorrow, and no more death — only the incredible wonder of his love.

FAMILY BONDS

We called my sister Jane a "scaredy cat." As a child, she feared germs, intruders, and bad food. She washed her hands till they shriveled, pulled the curtains every evening at dusk, and sniffed everything before it touched her mouth.

As an adult, her terror shifted to leaving home, traveling on trains, heavy traffic, and big cities — specifically Chicago. Nonetheless, she took on all those challenges to be with me when I was hospitalized with acute leukemia. "What's gotten into Jane?" our other sisters asked in amazement. "She's scared of everything. How did she dare do this?"

Bottom line? Jane cared more about me than her own safety. Her love transcended her fears as she packed her bags, boarded the Amtrak in Lafayette, Indiana, navigated the busy streets of Chicago, and found her way through the hospital maze to my side.

Her love also lifted me above my fears. Somehow the surgical insert of a PICC line in my upper arm to administer chemotherapy wasn't so bad with Jane's hand to grab, the side-effects of toxic drugs like Daunorubicin and Cytarabine not so debilitating as Jane fetched me hot tea, the long nights more bearable knowing Jane would be there in the morning.

Family love isn't perfect. Sometimes we siblings argue and separate. Sometimes we badmouth each other. Sometimes we just ignore each other. We get busy and life moves on. Then something like cancer threatens our lives, and we find in a new way that people who matter most are people who know us best and love us anyway. And, like God, they love us far more than we believed possible.

Family love is not limited to people with biological connections. Some of my most precious sisters and brothers are related to me in Christ. That bond is so strong that when one member of our family is struck down by illness, the rest of the family feels it as one. We reach out to each other with prayers, cards, meals, visits, and offers to help in any way possible. And because we're family, we accept the help and give God thanks for it.

Cancer cannot cripple that kind of love.

WELCOME THE DAY

A friend's son, who had Down's syndrome, greeted every day the same. He'd yank open the blinds on the patio doors and announce:

"This is the day that the Lord has made;
we will rejoice and be glad in it!"

Not all of us have that kind of zest for life. There are some days we'd rather dismiss from our calendars. We'd like to pull the covers over our heads and let the day pass without us. Other days we'd like to rush through, hoping for something better on the other side.

It takes something like cancer to freeze-frame us in the present. For when the dreaded news comes, we realize we no longer have the luxury of wasting time griping about piddly stuff like bad weather or boring weekends or wrinkly foreheads. All that stuff that we used to fret over becomes inconsequential when the future is in jeopardy and all we're sure we have is today.

Worrying about the future is inevitable, of course, as our lives take a detour from the ordinary into a bizarre maze of tests, surgical procedures, blood work, and treatment options. We don't know what's coming next, and that bothers us. Not knowing if we're doing the right thing also bothers us: Are we seeing the right doctor? Are we getting the best treatment for our type of cancer?

But most of all we worry about how much time we have left. What are my chances of living with this cancer — will I live to see my son graduate from college? My daughter get married? Will I be well enough to plan a vacation, finish a work project, pay off the mortgage on the house? What will my family do without me?

Psalm 90:12 tells us, "Teach us to number our days aright, that we may gain a heart of wisdom." In many ways, cancer is a wake-up call that tells us we must stop worrying about a future that we cannot control and a past that is already behind us. It is a reminder to start thinking about what really matters. It is a mandate to boot ourselves out of the recliner of sorrow and self-pity, grab hold of healing, and get back to work.

It is a mandate to love each day because, no matter what it brings, God gives us *this* day and he will be with us in it.

> *Satisfy us in the morning with your unfailing love,*
> *that we may sing for joy and be glad all our days.*
>
> PSALM 90:14

> *I trust in you, O LORD;*
> *I say, "You are my God."*
> *My times are in your hands.*
>
> PSALM 31:14 – 15

> *Jesus said, "Do not worry about tomorrow, for tomorrow*
> *will worry about itself. Each day has enough trouble of its own."*
>
> MATTHEW 6:34

THE JOY OF WORK

For weeks prior to being diagnosed with leukemia, I had such low blood counts that the doctor ordered me to stay out of crowds. I couldn't go to a shopping mall, a restaurant, and most painful of all — church. What kept me sane during that time was going to work.

Work was therapeutic; it kept me on task when my mind threatened to fracture in all directions, chasing "what ifs": What if it's an autoimmune disease like lupus? What if it's a funky virus? What if it's cancer? Work kept me busy during the drag time of waiting for the doctor to call. And it allowed me to screen out the calls of well-meaning friends and family who pressed for updates.

Work also helped me transition back to health. It was a kind of turning point from the abnormal world of cancer — surgery, hospitalization, treatment, and recovery — to the normal rhythm of life: getting up with the alarm, hitting the treadmill, breakfast, devotions, then off to work.

God designed us to work, whether it's in a business suit, sweat-pants, uniform, or jeans. Long before sin entered Paradise, God took Adam "and put him in the Garden of Eden to work it and take care of it." Tending God's good creation — work — was a part of the perfect order of things.

Sure, sin took its toll on work; after the Fall, work became "painful toil." As a result work doesn't always feel like Paradise to us. Sometimes it feels like an avalanche of unfinished projects, a tightrope of interpersonal conflict, a murky cloud of expectations. But if it's truly the work that God has called us to do, then he will help us do it. And we will find goodness and fulfillment in it.

A man can do nothing better than to eat and drink and find satisfaction in his work. This, too, I see, is from the hand of God.

ECCLESIASTES 2:24

CANCER IS SO LIMITED

It cannot shatter hope

FINDING A DOCTOR

Three months after treatment, my lymphoma recurred. While agonizing over this with Ed, a fellow non-Hodgkin's survivor, he said, "You really ought to see my doctor at Northwestern."

"Maybe I'll do that," I said. But privately I dismissed the suggestion as I had several times before. Why should I drive an hour into Chicago for treatment when I could get it through an oncologist less than five minutes from my house?

Still, treatment options were narrowing. So on the way home, I thought, "You really ought to pray about this." Two days later I was at work when I had the urge to call Ed's doctor. I tried to blow it off, but the thought kept coming back. So I finally sighed, called Ed, got the contact numbers, and called the doctor.

The first time I met Dr. Leo Gordon, I knew I was in good hands. In addition to his world-renown reputation in research, testing, and teaching, this man really cared. He had plowed through a dozen years of reports, scans, and notes on me. Now he asked in-depth questions about my medical history. He did a complete physical exam, verifying lumps I had felt myself plus others that had eluded my probing fingers. Then he connected the dots in my complicated case and made recommendations for further treatment.

Remember the little slave girl who cared about her master, Naaman, enough to suggest a healer for his leprosy? "If only my master would see the prophet who is in Samaria! He would cure him of his leprosy," the little girl told Naaman's wife (2 Kings 5:3). Amazingly, Naaman listened to the little girl, traveled to another country to see a prophet he had never heard of, and was cured.

Doctors don't heal us, of course; only God can do that. But God can and does use physicians in this world to effect that healing. And when we ask for guidance in finding the right doctor, God may answer us through suggestions of others — like Ed, who finally nagged me into listening — and receiving — God's direction. And the God of all hope led me to a doctor who has given me hope for healing in my journey with cancer.

May the God of hope fill you with all joy
and peace as you trust in him, so that you may overflow
with hope by the power of the Holy Spirit.

ROMANS 15:13

But now, Lord, what do I look for?
My hope is in you.

PSALM 39:7

Do not be anxious about anything,
but in everything, by prayer and petition, with thanksgiving,
present your requests to God.

PHILIPPIANS 4:6

WAITING FOR RESULTS

Cindy was one year removed from her battle with ovarian cancer when her CA – 125 (tumor marker) rose above normal. Her doctor reacted quickly, ordering CT-scans, then a needle biopsy. While waiting for the results, my friend seemed unnaturally calm. "Aren't you going nuts, waiting for the doctor to call?" I asked her.

"Well, sure," she said. "It's hard to wait. But on the other hand, this gives me more time to hope that I don't have cancer again."

Sometimes not knowing is better than knowing. It's the between time when we can hug the slimmest of chances that we don't have cancer, or that it's been caught very early, or that it hasn't jumped the fence into another part of our body. It's a time when we can tell ourselves that maybe the blood test was an anomaly, or the little bump in our groin is an ingrown hair, or the blob of white on the mammogram is just a cyst. It's a time when we can say, "I've never felt better in my life — I can't have cancer!"

But, as another friend, Diane, said about her recurrent breast cancer: "Our gut tells us we have it." So the waiting, like so many other things about cancer, becomes a mind game. Part of us says that the doctor wouldn't be ordering all those tests if he didn't suspect cancer, and part of us argues that he's just being thorough. Caught in that tension, we lose our focus in conversation. Food loses its appeal. We're exhausted but we can't sleep. Our minds race ahead of the doctor's call, projecting possibilities.

By nature we don't do waiting well — whether it's waiting for something good or bad. Abraham and Sarah chafed while waiting for a baby. Job, with all his losses — possessions, children, and health — fretted about God's failure to speak. The disciples nodded off while waiting with Jesus who was agonizing over his coming death. But none of that chafing or fretting or nodding off has any effect on the final report.

Hoping for good results on a biopsy helps make the waiting a bit more bearable. But even better is using the waiting time to cling to God, knowing that nothing in life is more important than that. It's also trusting that he already holds those test results in his hands, and that because we belong to him, everything will somehow work together for good.

> *I will praise the LORD, who counsels me;*
> *even at night my heart instructs me.*
> *I have set the LORD always before me.*
> *Because he is at my right hand,*
> *I will not be shaken.*
>
> PSALM 16:7 – 8

> *In repentance and rest is your salvation,*
> *in quietness and trust is your strength.*
>
> ISAIAH 30:15

21

Who of you by worrying can add a single hour to his life? Since you cannot do this very little thing, why do you worry about the rest?

LUKE 12:25 – 26

Always choose hope. If you have been told that your time is limited, believe that life can still be a fulfilling adventure. Choose to live to the very fullest, discovering that every day is a good and perfect gift in spite of the circumstances.

GREG ANDERSON

Life in God's reign is kaleidoscopic in nature. We try in vain to picture life's next scene, while grace is at work resetting the stage.

PHILIP GULLEY

Schedule all your worrying for a specific half-hour about the middle of the day. Then take a nap during this period. God aims to exalt himself by working for those who wait for him.

JOHN PIPER

Getting through Chemo

When I was diagnosed with lymphoma, I jumped at the opportunity to be treated with Rituxan; a kind of smart bomb that boosts the effectiveness of the immune system. Leaving healthy cells alone, the drug seeks out cancer cells, attaches itself to them, and detonates them. Years later, I also welcomed Zevalin, which binds radioactive isotopes to Rituxan, turning it into a kind of nuclear warhead against cancer.

I was less enthusiastic when I was diagnosed with acute leukemia and found myself hooked up to bags of drugs so lethal that nurses had to wear gloves, gowns, and glasses to tend the stuff dripping into my veins. One time my IV broke, leaving a puddle of red stuff on the floor. I had to be quarantined and my room sealed off until a sheathed crew could clean up the spill.

But I felt downright rebellious some mornings when I had to reach for little doses of chemo and put them into my mouth. I hated their debilitating side effects: nausea, headaches, mouth sores, gritty eyes, bone pain, and overwhelming fatigue. I hated how they shrouded my spirit, graying out a world I have always enjoyed in full color. I hated how they made me weepy, irritable, and impatient with people's shortcomings — especially my own.

When I wanted to toss the drugs down the disposal, though, I thought of how drugs had already beat my leukemia into remission, and how they were keeping it from roaring back. What's more, they were a kind of guard dog against recurring lymphoma. So I got two-for-one protection from a handful of pills every morning.

We don't have to like treatment in order for it to work. But we should hope that it will work for us, destroying the cancer that threatens our lives. Otherwise we'll never get through it.

People in Jesus' day didn't always like their treatment options, either. The crippled man must have screamed inside as his friends dropped him through a roof to land at the feet of Jesus. The woman with incurable bleeding was so fear-bound that she touched Jesus from the back, then disappeared into the crowd.

And the man with demons begged Jesus not to cast his tormentors into a bottomless pit. Yet all made it through treatment because they trusted the One who healed them through it.

Cancer cannot shatter that kind of hope.

Wait for the LORD;
be strong and take heart
and wait for the LORD.

PSALM 27:14

My flesh and my heart may fail,
but God is the strength of my heart,
and my portion forever.

PSALM 73:26

If I'm taking a pill every morning that my doctor says will greatly reduce the chances of a recurrence, it's probably helpful if I believe that. Side effects can be nasty, so if I'm going to suffer then I had better believe the treatment is worth it.

MARY ANN, BREAST CANCER SURVIVOR

REACHING FOR REMISSION

*L*ook at this verse," my daughter, Laura, said to me, holding up her teacher's manual for vacation Bible school. "How am I supposed to teach *that* to third graders?"

She showed me Matthew 26:28 (KJV): "For this is my blood of the new testament, which is shed for many for the remission of sins." *Testament* wasn't a problem, she said; it was *remission* that seemed too hard for young minds to grasp.

Remission is also difficult for people with cancer to grasp. In the biblical sense, "remission of sins" means "forgiveness of sins." It means that through the blood of Christ, full payment has been made for our sins. That doesn't mean we'll never have to struggle with sin again. As long as we live here on earth, our new, pardoned selves will battle against our old, flesh-bound natures.

Likewise, the most that many of us with cancer can hope for is remission. Medically that means that through surgery, chemotherapy, radiation — whatever — our cancer will be knocked back so far that no trace of the disease can be detected.

But remission does not mean lifetime freedom from cancer. We will be fighting cancer for a very long time — if not physically, then emotionally. Every time we get a cold, our hip aches, we feel dizzy, and our fears whisper *cancer,* we'll have to lift up arms against the enemy.

Physically, we might have to battle cancer again, too. Years ago, doctors assumed that if you lived five years without a recurrence, you were cured of cancer. That's no longer true of many cancers. A friend, Mary, proved that when she had a recurrence twenty years after she was "cured" of breast cancer. Another's melanoma metastasized to the brain fifteen years after a complete remission.

As my daughter says, "Cancer doesn't obey any rules."

Nonetheless, *remission* is a powerful incentive for people with cancer. It means that all we've endured to get rid of cancer has succeeded — at least for now. Maybe it'll be gone forever; maybe not. Meantime, we live from day to day in God's grace, rejoicing for the reprieve and thanking him for this healing — and the next — until one day we stand before Christ, forever cured of cancer.

> *The LORD is my strength and my shield;*
> *my heart trusts in him, and I am helped.*
>
> **PSALM 28:7**

God does not always take us out of problematic situations, but He gives us the peace we seek as we proceed prayerfully through each experience.

H. NORMAN WRIGHT

There is no medicine like hope, no incentive so great, and no tonic so powerful as expectation of something better tomorrow.

ORISON SWETT MARDEN

CANCER IS SO LIMITED

It cannot corrode faith

VISION OF HOPE

*P*eople in the church in which I grew up didn't have visions. So when as a young married mom I found myself at one of the lowest points in my life and cried out to God, offering him my life because I couldn't manage it anymore, the last thing I expected was a vision. Nonetheless, that's what happened. Some time between awareness and sleep, I saw Jesus.

He didn't say a word; he just looked at me. And the look of love was so tender, so understanding, so *mine,* that it grabbed me by the heart. I knew with absolute certainty, from that moment on, that I was a child of God.

I thought of people in the Bible who'd had dreams or visions. Joseph dreamed of a future time when he'd rule over his cruel brothers. Saul had a vision of Christ that turned his life upside down, aborting his plans to persecute Christians and transforming him into one of their staunchest leaders. John had a revelation, too, of God's triumph over Satan and his eternal reign with the people he loves.

But that was the Bible. Personally, I knew of no one who'd had such a revelation. So I wondered at the time why God would give me a vision. Yes, it encouraged me at a time when I needed it; yes, it assured me that Christ was my Savior; and, yes, it strengthened my faith in God.

But it did something more, too. Over the years I have come to realize that without absolute affirmation of Christ's abiding love, I would have had a terrible time getting through the rough patches that were to come.

I could not have predicted that I would have four kinds of cancer in the coming years; I might have lost heart had I known. But God led me, strengthening me as I learned to walk with him and proving to me many times how he would go with me, nourishing and sustaining me. So when the evil days of cancer did come upon me, I could reach for Christ, knowing that he would carry me through.

While I am thankful for it, we don't need a vision to assure us of Christ's redeeming love for us. What Jesus said to his disciples in Matthew 28:20 applies to us today as well: "Surely I am with you always, to the very end of the age." We who trust in Jesus will find him with us no matter where we go or what problems we face. We have his Word on that.

> Unless the LORD had given me help,
> I would soon have dwelt in the silence of death.
> When I said, "My foot is slipping,"
> your love, O LORD, supported me.
> When anxiety was great within me,
> your consolation brought joy to my soul.

PSALM 94:17 – 19

Losing your job, your health, or a dream. Living and dying. They are all opportunities to respond to God's love.

M. CRAIG BARNES

ASKING HARD QUESTIONS

God doesn't always answer our prayer to rid us of cancer. He can, of course, if he chooses to do so. But when he doesn't, we can drift out of the calm waters of faith into a whirlpool of confusion.

My friend Diane hit that troubled water when her ovarian cancer recurred. "Why didn't God heal me?" asked this stalwart woman of faith, who suddenly sounded like a lost child. She and others at her church had prayed fervently that she would be healed of cancer. She had even met with the elders, who anointed her with oil and prayed over her. And when her next CA – 125 (tumor marker for cancer) dropped into the normal range, we rejoiced with her and gave thanks to God.

The good news had barely gotten round when the CA – 125 started rising again. My friend couldn't help asking: *Why didn't God answer the prayers of so many people? Why did he allow the cancer to come back? Why does he heal some and not others? Where is God when we need him? Are we guilty of some secret sin that God is now disciplining us for with disease?*

There are no easy answers to such "whys." What is comforting, though, is that God does not forbid us from asking. Job, David, and Jesus himself asked hard questions about suffering, and were not discouraged from doing so. We may even get glimpses of the answer to why we have cancer: perhaps to give us time and the impetus to restore relationships with family, to shift our priorities in life, to help us appreciate each day, to see health as a gift, to reach out to others in need.

But the greatest response to such questions is to turn our eyes away from ourselves and lift them to God. Then, like Job, we'll see God as the one who laid the foundations of the earth, shut up the sea behind doors, who gives orders to the morning, tips over the water jars of the heavens — and yet is with us, responding to our every need, and saying, "Fear not, for I have redeemed you; I have summoned you by name; you are mine. When you pass through the waters, I will be with you; and when you pass through the rivers, they will not sweep over you" (Isaiah 43:1 − 2).

God, our Creator, Redeemer, and Comforter is with us in the whys, the why nots, the remissions, and the recurrences of cancer. His presence is the answer to every question.

> *As a father has compassion on his children,*
> *so the LORD has compassion on those who fear him;*
> *for he knows how we are formed,*
> *he remembers that we are dust.*
>
> PSALM 103:13 − 14

In order to suffer without dwelling on our own affliction, we must think about a greater affliction, and turn to Christ on the Cross.

THOMAS MERTON

DOWN TO OUR HAIR

wo weeks from the day I had my first infusion of chemo, my hair fell out. I had been warned, of course. But secretly I cherished the hope that my thick locks would defy the statistics, clinging to my scalp despite the red stuff dripping into my veins.

A volunteer barber at the hospital had suggested that if I shampooed less often and used a wide-toothed comb, I would keep my hair. I tried both. But when I began shedding like an unkempt dog all over my pajamas, pillows, and bathroom floor, I recognized the inevitable. I called a friend from work who suggested clipping my hair back to two inches so that going bald would be less traumatic. She came to my hospital room and began buzzing.

The snappy do lasted about two days. One morning in the shower, I watched in horror as water washed off shampoo, and clumps of hair that gathered around my feet. When I looked in the mirror, all I saw were stray wisps and a shiny scalp. I was undeniably, irrefutably bald. And there wasn't a thing I could do about it.

Samson woke up one morning minus his hair and his strength and all sense of control. Perhaps we feel a bit like that as well when we first confront our naked scalps. We can't trust our bodies anymore, we can't trust our strength. We can't even trust hair to grow on our head.

But we can trust God. Because no matter what happens to us, God, the creator and ruler of the universe, the one who made the great creatures of the deep and flung stars all over the heavens, is in control. He controls the tides of the oceans and the wind in the trees. He controls the tiny little birds that ride the colors of dawn.

We need not be afraid of what is happening to us because God is in control. He is so in control that, as Luke 12:7 tells us, he counts the very hairs of our head. Imagine that! Every hair that washes down the drain the morning you go bald has God's number on it. Every wisp that straggles upward from your scalp after treatment ends has God's number on it.

If God cares that much about the hair on your head, you can trust that he cares for you. And nothing — not even cancer — can separate you from his loving control.

Doubt not His grace because of thy tribulation, but believe that He loveth thee as much in seasons of trouble as in times of happiness.

CHARLES SPURGEON

All men are like grass,
and all their glory is like the flowers of the field.
The grass withers and the flowers fall,
but the word of our God stands forever.

ISAIAH 40:6,8

He watches us with fatherly care, keeping all creatures under his control, so that not one of the hairs on our heads (for they are numbered) nor even a little bird can fall to the ground without the will of our Father.

THE BELGIC CONFESSION, ARTICLE 13

The art of living lies less in eliminating our troubles than in growing with them.

BERNARD M. BARUCH

I have held many things in my hands, and I have lost them all; but whatever I have placed in God's hands, that I still possess.

MARTIN LUTHER

ANOTHER FINISH LINE

I used to keep a log of chemo treatments, complete with blood test results and side effects. It was a handy little reference tool, especially when the doctor wanted to delay a treatment because my white count was too low. "It was lower three months ago and you gave me the treatment!" I said, after consulting my chart. He checked his records and okayed the chemo.

But the most beneficial aspect of the chart was its visual assurance of how I was progressing toward the finish line. "I'm a third of the way through treatment," I'd say. Soon it was half-way, then three-quarters. Then I was sprinting through the final session.

Well, not exactly sprinting. Dragging, was more like it. I was so wiped out that I could fall asleep while eating supper. I could barely make it through a workday on eight hours of sleep a night, so I'd crash on the weekends, refueling on ten-to twelve-hour stretches of snooze.

Mary Lou, who had breast cancer before I did, smiled when I asked her how long it would take to recover. "Double the time you had chemo; that's how long it will be before you feel completely healthy again," she said.

That advice was oddly comforting. It took the pressure off trying to force recovery in too brief a time. It also allowed me to slow down a little to enjoy signs of returning health, like incisions that began fading from red to pink, having more energy left at the end of the day, finding food appetizing again, enjoying a morning run.

When we get sick, our bodies yearn to return to health. So when we give them rest, fluids, good food, exercise, regular checkups, and plenty of spiritual nourishment, we can trust God to renew our strength, as he promises in Isaiah 40:31.

We can have faith that one day cancer will be behind us and we will be healthy again — if not here, then in the life to come.

Those who hope in the LORD
will renew their strength.
They will soar on wings like eagles;
they will run and not grow weary,
they will walk and not be faint.

ISAIAH 40:31

Although the world is full of suffering, it is also full of the over-coming of it.

HELEN KELLER

A faith central to everyday life can be strong medicine, a medicine of which we doctors should be more aware and encourage whenever possible.

SIDNEY J. WINAWER, M.D.

It is my desire that survivors will one day feel proud of having had cancer, and that others will come to regard it . . . as a "gritty badge of distinction."

SUSAN NESSIM & JUDITH ELLIS

CANCER IS SO LIMITED

It cannot destroy peace

SURVIVAL STATISTICS

*Y*ou're gonna be okay," whispered the lady in pink, as she wheeled me down the hall. "Eighty percent of breast lumps aren't cancer."

I stifled a sigh. So far, statistics had not been in my favor. So why, years after surviving a mastectomy and treatment for breast cancer, was I still drawn to survival statistics like a moth to a lamp, especially after hearing that a fellow survivor had recurred? The volunteer's prediction wasn't accurate, either; I *did* have breast cancer.

My breast lump, which was big enough to be seen by the naked eye, hadn't shown up on a mammogram. Mammograms are effective only 80 percent of the time.

The size of my lump plus five positive nodes drove down my five-year survival rate to less than 25 percent. What's more, I, like so many other cancer survivors, had learned how senseless statistics were in forecasting survival. As one doctor said, "Maybe only 10 percent of patients with your type and stage of cancer are cured, but within that 10 percent, your odds are zero percent or 100 percent."

So what drove me to statistics? Perhaps it's the kind of fear that drove King Saul to consult a medium on the eve of a battle that would later claim his life (1 Samuel 28). God was not answering the king through dreams or other prophets, so Saul tried to conjure up the spirit of Samuel to tell him what to do. Saul got a message all right, but it knocked him to the ground.

Cancer knocks us to the ground, too. Still, rather than running to statistics (or doctors that quote them) to ease our fears, we should trust in our Heavenly Father, who alone knows how long we will live. The Almighty God, who created us and sent his Son to die for us so that we might be delivered from the curse of sin, determines the exact number of our days and sets limits we cannot exceed (Job 14:5).

Instead of focusing on death, we should, as Deuteronomy 30 says, choose life — that we may love the Lord our God, listen to his voice, and hold fast to his assurance that, by Christ's wounds, we will be healed.

The LORD will keep you from all harm —
he will watch over your life;
the LORD will watch over your coming and going
both now and forevermore.

PSALM 121:7 – 8

Be aware that the diagnosis of cancer is not necessarily a sentence of death. There are millions of people in the United States to whom cancer is now a memory.

HAROLD H. BENJAMIN

Now we know that if the earthly tent we live in is destroyed,
we have a building from God,
an eternal house in heaven, not built by human hands.

2 CORINTHIANS 5:1

FACING SURGERY

*F*acing surgery can be terrifying. Images begin cluttering your mind. You're going under the knife — what if the surgeon who wields it had a bad night and isn't fully up to the task? You'll be totally paralyzed under anesthetic — or will you? What if you wake up in the middle of the operation? What if you never wake up?

The pre-surgical consult doesn't help, either. Though doctors and nurses try to assure you that none of these complications will happen to you, their litany of surgical risks invites your mind to scramble down trails of terror.

Then, too, there's the unsettling ritual of checking in the day of the surgery: taking off everything that's familiar, including glasses, rings, and watch; dumping them into a plastic bag branded with the name of the hospital; and donning a faded green garment with ties in the back.

You and your spouse read a psalm together as you wait for the gurney that will take you into the operating room. "I love the LORD, for he heard my voice; he heard my cry for mercy. Because he turned his ear to me, I will call on him as long as I live . . ." (Psalm 116:1 – 2). You pray together. Then the pastor arrives. He opens his Bible to read — the same psalm that you've just read! Clearly the words are a custom fit for you.

For someone who has fasted at least twelve hours before surgery, hasn't had a sip of water for hours, hasn't slept well since the doctor reported the biopsy results, and who can't help role-playing what may happen in surgery, the words of Scripture are a feast. They're the bread of life and living water and balm in Gilead, and all those other metaphors we've read in the Bible for so many years but have just now come alive to us. They are Christ to us, calming our restlessness and giving us peace.

The best preparation for surgery isn't bodily fitness, but soul fitness. When we have the peace of God, which passes all understanding, we can face any operation with confidence.

BATTLING INSOMNIA

There is nothing longer than a night of insomnia. You fall exhausted into sleep, then wake up and chase the clock around the dial. It's too early to get up — the darkness of the room hasn't lifted at all, but you're tired of turning round and round in bed — and deep breathing and other relaxation exercises aren't working. You could take a pill, but then you'd be wiped out for the day.

Into the wasteland of exhaustion creep restless thoughts: anxiety about a work project, guilt about not having sent someone a card, fears about an upcoming appointment with the doctor. You know the intensity of those reactions is distorted, but when you're weary to the bone, everything seems out of control. You feel assaulted by the devil himself.

Insomnia often comes with cancer. Long nights of interrupted sleep may start after you find out you have the disease, be exacerbated by surgery, and be intensified by ongoing chemotherapy.

Once you have insomnia, it can feed on itself, turning every night into an endurance trial.

A sleep specialist can help. Mine offered suggestions such as cutting back on caffeine, restricting fluids after supper, going to bed and getting up at the same time every day, and avoiding anything stimulating for an hour before bed. But what really helped me was her assurance that my sleep problem would ease once I was done with chemotherapy.

Knowing the problem was temporary helped me view sleeplessness a new way. Rather than fighting it, I began entrusting the time to God. Into the quiet darkness came the names of individuals to pray for, situations to sort through, hymns of praise, verses of Scripture. In time, I even learned another dimension of Jesus' promise: "Come to me, all you who are weary and burdened, and I will give you rest" (Matthew 11:28).

Resting in Christ is better than sleep. It offers you the kind of peace that transcends understanding (Philippians 4:7) and makes even the darkest, longest night brighten with the presence of God.

By day the LORD directs his love,
at night his song is with me —
a prayer to the God of my life.

PSALM 42:8

Weeping may remain for a night,
but rejoicing comes in the morning.

PSALM 30:5

Jesus said, "Come to me, all you who are weary and burdened, and I
will give you rest. Take my yoke upon you and learn from me, for I am
gentle and humble in heart, and you will find rest for your souls."

MATTHEW 11:28 – 29

There is no cry so good as that which comes from the bottom of
the mountains; no prayer half so hearty as that which comes up
from the depths of the soul, through deep trials and afflictions.
For they bring us to God, and we are happier; for nearness to
God is happiness.

CHARLES SPURGEON

REST AND RECOVERY

*T*oday, hospitals are for really sick people. As soon as you're out of crisis you're in a wheelchair and out the door. You're still dangling drains that need to be tended every few hours, you have to stop at the local pharmacy to fill prescriptions for pain killers, and you need help getting out of the car and into the house. When you get inside, you collapse into a recliner and pull up the afghan.

Sitting still for long stretches of time is a trial when you're feeling good. We're up with the alarm to take a morning run, and rushing through shower and breakfast so we can be out the door on time. Then we're snaking through traffic to work, where we hang up our jacket, turn on the computer, check into voice mail, and take instructions from our DayTimer. The days pass in a blur.

When recovering from cancer surgery or treatment, however, we have to rest. Rest is essential for the body to repair itself. It's also a great time to feed our souls.

Some of my best times with God were during the days following surgery, when I spent long hours reading Scripture, journaling, talking to friends, taking walks, and praying. I had nowhere to go, no one I had to see, nothing that had to be done. Life was on hold. I could just bask in the lovely, wide-open spaces of healing. I was Mary instead of Martha, sitting at the feet of Jesus and soaking up his teaching instead of rushing about in the kitchen.

Unfortunately, it sometimes takes a crisis to put the brakes on our frantic rush through life. God created us all with a need for rest, for nightly repair of the cells and muscles that we have used during the day. At the very beginning of creation, God recommended that we set aside one day a week to find rest in him. So when we meet with other believers on Sunday to worship and praise God, we are refreshed and renewed for another week of work.

We can also build mini-Sabbaths into every day by setting aside an hour or two to meet with God in prayer, devotions, and Bible study. Or we can simply sit in silence before him, waiting for him to speak. If we do that, perhaps our lives won't become so frantic that it takes something like cancer to show us what really matters.

Find rest, O my soul, in God alone;
my hope comes from him.
He alone is my rock and my salvation;
he is my fortress, I will not be shaken.

PSALM 62:5 – 6

May God himself, the God of peace,
sanctify you through and through.

1 THESSALONIANS 5:23

My friends say they have come to appreciate their illnesses. Time in bed, in the hospital, and at home, and the care of medical attendants and family have helped them discover new values, develop a deeper faith in God, and grow in love and compassion.

MILDRED TENGBOM

CANCER IS SO LIMITED

It cannot kill friendship

WHAT FRIENDS ARE FOR

When my friend Karen was dumped by her husband, not all of her friends understood what she was going through. Some asked pretty insensitive questions about the failing marriage. Karen didn't need people like that when her heart was breaking.

"I have found it necessary during times like these to surround myself with supportive people," she told me.

People say pretty strange things about cancer, too, like, "You don't *look* like you have cancer." (How do you respond to that?) Or, "You must be very special for God to be putting you through this." (As Tevye said to God in *Fiddler on the Roof*, "Couldn't you choose someone else?") Or, "Oh, well; we're all going to die of something someday." (So just forget about the cancer, right?)

People who've just been diagnosed with cancer don't need explanations or rationalizations or even Scripturalizations — at least not initially, when minds and emotions are a thick, dark soup. We need the quiet support of someone like George, who told me months after I was diagnosed, "There are two people I pray for every day — you and Pauline" (another cancer survivor).

We need people like Mary, who told me one day when I confided that I was so weary that I couldn't focus — even on prayer: "When you're too tired or discouraged to pray, ask *us* to do it. That's what friends are for."

We need people like Diane and Ed and Cindy and Louie and countless other cancer survivors who are willing to walk the journey with us, comparing notes on prognosis, treatments, side effects, and questions of faith.

What's incredible is that I don't seek these people out; God sends them to me. When I feel especially needy and go looking for help, I don't always get what I need. But when I come to God first, begging for his wisdom and guidance, he provides exactly what I need. He puts flesh on those answers, sending me friends who, by God's Spirit, sense my heartaches: friends who listen without judgment when I need to vent; friends who seek me out when I have retreated in self-pity; friends who advocate for me when I'm too tired to do that for myself.

Cancer cannot kill that kind of friendship.

There is a friend who sticks closer than a brother.

PROVERBS 18:24

Jesus said, "I was sick and you looked after me."

MATTHEW 25:36

Rather than running from people when illness overtakes you, you need to seek them — selectively. There may not be enough time left for shallow relationships. Choose the people you really wish to be with.

AL B. WEIR, M.D.

Not everybody can handle emotions in a way that is helpful to you. Know that. Forgive that. Learn to overlook that. And seek out the people who are strong, someone you can lean on emotionally.

RUSTY FREEMAN

FELLOW SURVIVOR

Walking with cancer can be lonely. In addition to long stretches of waiting — to see the doctor, to have a bone scan, to get blood drawn — there are long nights of sleeplessness. Everyone else is zoned out, and you're pacing the dark with your thoughts. Then, too, there are those long stretches of recovery, when your world is limited to the couch or the bed.

Jesus knew loneliness, too. He traveled with twelve men for more than three years, yet most failed to grasp the point of his parables or to understand the true intent of his mission. Crowds of people asked for miracles, and bread, and other earthly things, ignoring his teaching about a heavenly kingdom. That must have made him feel lonely.

He was also challenged by the morally uptight leaders of his time, who questioned his methods of helping others. No matter that the blind had their sight restored or the lame were walking; Jesus was violating the Law by healing on the Sabbath and daring to tell people that their sins were forgiven. Surely Jesus felt lonely during those times, particularly when no one stepped forward to defend him.

He must have felt lonely praying in the Garden of Gethsemane, too, when his disciples nodded off while he struggled with his impending death. But he must have felt most lonely when God left him alone on the cross. "My God, my God, why hast thou forsaken me?" he cried out.

There is no aspect of loneliness that Jesus has not experienced, and so he truly understands everything that we are suffering. He's there for us when we feel most abandoned. We reach for him, and he comes to us — in his Word, in the lyrics of a song, in a card or call that lifts our spirits. He's present in the signs of healing in our body, and every encouraging test result. He's with us in the waiting and in the dark.

And he's present in himself. As the old hymn says, "He walks with us and talks with us and tells us we are his own." We are never alone when Jesus is our Friend.

He was pierced for our transgressions,
he was crushed for our iniquities;
the punishment that brought us peace was upon him,
and by his wounds we are healed.

ISAIAH 53:5

People brought all their sick to [Jesus] and begged him to let the sick
just touch the edge of his cloak, and all who touched him were healed.

MATTHEW 14:35 – 36

Jesus said, "Surely I am with you always, to the very end of the age."

MATTHEW 28:20

I have held many things in my hands, and I have lost them all;
but whatever I have placed in God's hands, that I still possess.

MARTIN LUTHER

If you don't already have one, get an answering machine. Your
private life is about to become everyone's reason to reach out
and touch you.

EMILY, BREAST CANCER SURVIVOR

RESTORED RELATIONSHIP

Donna was a power teacher. She inspired me to write in high school, not just by showing how, but by telling me I had a gift and encouraging me to use it. Her support was a lifeline both in and out of college. It kept me scribbling even when I had long ceased to think of writing as a profession. Eventually, her belief in me sent me on to graduate school, where I earned a master's degree in Communications. I eventually went on to a career in writing and editing.

Still, I hadn't seen my high school teacher in forty years. After a class reunion, I finally decided to call her. She would remember me, I was sure, but how would she respond? Our intense friendship that had developed during those years in high school had been a mixed cup; it had inspired me, but it had also broken me. I wasn't sure exactly how to process that experience. So, for years I had stored it high on a closet shelf, wrapped in fear.

Cancer gives you chutzpah, a friend once told me. It brings you

to the edge of life, then threatens to push you
over a cliff. You either fall, crashing on the
rocks below, or you learn to fly like an eagle.
I chose to flap my wings, and with that choice
came the courage to deal with unfinished business.

So one day, I called Donna.

"I've wanted to talk to you — for years!" she said. I had
tea with her that afternoon. We blew the dust of the years off of
our relationship, and with it, a lot of fear. And we reconciled,
not as student and teacher, but as two adults with life stories to
share. In the forty years since we had last seen each other, we'd
each been tested by adversity (Proverbs 17:17). Through the
intense heat of experiences such as cancer and personal loss, we
had drawn closer to the Lord, who had refined us and now
called us to work through our differences.

Rather than killing friendship, cancer can make us more appre-
ciative of the friends we have. It can also give us the chutzpah to
renew relationships with friends we haven't seen in years.

HEALING LAUGHTER

When a friend had a bad day, he'd top it off by catching a really sad movie and having a personal pity party.

I prefer a good laugh when things aren't going well. The movie *My Favorite Year* with Peter O'Toole makes me laugh out of control. So does *My Chauffer* with Deborah Foreman. The latest addition to my laugh file is *Calendar Girls,* a British film, which had me hooting in a hospital room. Books get me giggling, too, though I feel a bit silly laughing out loud when people around me can't share the joke.

I also cultivate friends who can be fun in any situation, even through cancer. They can laugh with me while trying on outrageous wigs or hats, join me in fabricating stories as we people-watch in a large waiting room, improvise escapes from hospital rooms, and rehearse evil things to do to the phlebotomist who fails to stick me the first time. As Proverbs 17:22 says, "A cheerful heart is good medicine."

Laughter is a communal thing. It pulls you out of yourself and toward others. Like a baby's smile, it prompts you to play along. An unexpected twist, a silly slip, a funny noise, a time of goofiness — all can break down barriers of fear and pain. Sure, it's escapism, but there are times when we all need to take a little whiff of laughing gas to rise above pain.

Laughter is also therapeutic. Many years ago Norman Cousins had a hunch that laughter helped him recover from a serious illness. Subsequent research has proved him right. Laughter helps us heal.

So hold on to your sense of humor. Use it like a smile to connect you with others. People who can laugh together have too much fun to give up on life.

There is a time for everything,
and a season for every activity under heaven . . .
a time to weep and a time to laugh.

ECCLESIASTES 3:1, 4

Encourage one another daily, as long as it is called Today.

HEBREWS 3:13

It has always seemed to me that hearty laughter is a good way to jog internally without having to go outdoors.

NORMAN COUSINS

Laughter is therapeutic. Somehow it gives me the emotional space I need to focus on the big picture.

CARLA, BREAST CANCER SURVIVOR

Laughter has much in common with prayer. In both acts, we stand on equal ground, freely acknowledging ourselves as fallen creatures. We take ourselves less seriously.

PHILIP YANCEY

The best moments any of us have as human beings are those moments when for a little while it is possible to escape the squirrel-cage of being *me* into the landscape of being *us*.

FREDERICK BUECHNER

Laughter is the best medicine for a long and happy life. He who laughs — lasts!

WILFRED A. PETERSON

CANCER IS SO LIMITED

It cannot shut out memories

MAKING THE MOST OF TIME

Goal setting is an essential part of battling cancer. Making it through chemo, finishing a quilt, writing a book, attending a family reunion, running a marathon — all are motivations to keep reaching, to keep trying. Another kind of encouragement to keep tromping through cancer is remembering how God has already granted us life extensions.

Thirteen years ago, when I was diagnosed with breast cancer, I prayed for enough time — just three years — to see my son start medical school and my daughter married. In the time since, my son has become a practicing emergency room doctor, and my daughter and son-in-law have given us three beautiful grandchildren. God granted me far more than I asked for.

What will I do with the time?

I think, sometimes, of Hezekiah, the good king of Judah, who wept when he realized he was dying. God granted him a fifteen-year extension. During that time the king showed off all his treasures to visiting envoys from Babylon. When the prophet Isaiah scolded Hezekiah, saying Babylon would later carry off all that treasure, plus Hezekiah's descendents, the king just sighed with relief, thinking, "There will be peace and security in my lifetime."

Indulging ourselves with clothes, toys, trips; showing off what we've accumulated, kicking back in relief, knowing that we're safe for a bit longer — is that what we do with a life extension? What is the Lord *really* calling us to do?

He may be simply calling us to get through one day at a time till we're healthy enough to resume former activities. Perhaps he wants us to spend more time with those who will survive us, building a lasting legacy of love. Maybe we just need to get over our preoccupation with ourselves so we can reach out and help someone else.

Whatever God's call is for you, treat each day as an opportunity — and a challenge — to extend a life worth living.

TIMES OF HEALING

When we're going through cancer, the world can close in on us, making us believe this is all there is. We can't think beyond the disease. We're bound by it, captive to its every whim. We fret about surgery. Then, when we recover from surgery, we're obsessed with treatment. When we finish chemo or radiation, we worry about recurrence. When the cancer does recur, we start estimating our chances for survival. Even when the threat is past, we don't feel safe.

We don't just have cancer; it has us.

When that happens, maybe it's time to look back. Like the Israelites of old, who needed to be reminded of how God had brought them out of slavery and through the wilderness into the Promised Land, we need to recall times of healing in our lives.

Remember when you had the flu? You coughed till your ribs ached, your head felt like it was under a rock, and your body was on fire. The doctor wouldn't give you an antibiotic because this was a viral infection, so you just toughed it out. Eventually you got better.

Or remember when you slipped on ice in the driveway and broke your leg? You had to shuffle around for six weeks in a cast, swinging your body between crutches. Driving, going up steps, walking through a parking lot — everything was a challenge. For the first time in your life, you appreciated the parking spaces and special seats reserved for people with handicaps. Finally, though, the cast came off, and you were back to walking again.

The body has a remarkable capacity to heal. Our very cells have the memory of health. Even when assaulted by trauma or disease, they *want* to return to normal. God, who designed us this way, wants more than physical health for us; he wants us to be whole — body, mind, and spirit.

Romans 1 tells us that we have, planted within our spirits, the knowledge of God. Sin, like cancer, tries to pervert that knowledge, but the farther we get from God, the more miserable we become. The only way to true healing is through God's Son, Jesus Christ. In him we find the kind of restoration for our souls and bodies that transcends all disease.

You restored me to health
and let me live.
Surely it was for my benefit
that I suffered such anguish.

ISAIAH 38:16 – 17

The human body is its own best apothecary and . . . the most successful prescriptions are those filled by the body itself.

NORMAN COUSINS

What I want my patients to focus on is getting well and what they can do about it, rather than to focus on the cancer and how to be sick.

HAROLD H. BENJAMIN

72

WHAT PEOPLE HAVE DONE

*F*riends at church brought meals to us after I got home from nearly a month's stay in the hospital. Homemade soup and rolls; a New Zealand Christmas feast of lamb, potatoes, fresh beans; fresh grilled salmon, rice, and a tossed salad; roast chicken, mashed potatoes, apple tarts — oh my! The memory of those meals still makes me gasp. Not only did that food tempt me into eating again; it also overwhelmed me. What generosity! What loving concern!

The cards I received were also spirit-lifters. Every day was a special occasion as I opened hand-addressed envelopes. I collected the beautiful cards and notes in a basket. Occasionally I read through them again, reflecting on how good people were to us in our time of need.

According to Ram Cnaan in *The Newer Deal: Social Work and Religion in Partnership*, it is the norm for churches in America to provide social services such as caring for the sick and needy.

Believers, whose model is Christ, reach out to others because it's the right thing to do. They only wish they could do more.

Sometimes, though, it's hard to be the recipient of such largesse. How can we possibly accept such gifts without returning them in kind? How can we thank people enough for their cooking, baking, transporting, mailings, prayers, and visits?

We can send thank-you notes, of course, but that's hardly enough. We can be so nourished and strengthened by their loving concern that we're able to join them once again in church activities. When we feel stronger, we can even respond to their example by providing meals for the next person in need.

But most of all, we can remember their gifts as symbolic of what Jesus Christ has done for us. When we were lost in sin, he gave his life for us, that we might be saved. We remember that and believe. And when we reach for the cup and bread of Communion to commemorate Christ's great gift to us, we also open ourselves up to the people who are eating and drinking with us. They, too, are the body and blood of Christ, given to us by Christ to nourish and feed us.

> *Let us consider how we may spur one another*
> *on toward love and good deeds.*
>
> HEBREWS 10:24

> *Whether you eat or drink or whatever you do,*
> *do it all for the glory of God.*
>
> 1 CORINTHIANS 10:31

Blessed are those who can give without remembering and take without forgetting.

ELIZABETH BIBESCO

We are not primarily
put on this earth to see
through one another, but
to see one another through.

PETER DE VRIES

UNEXPECTED KINDNESS

I once spent nearly six weeks waiting for results on an MRI that would determine whether or not my breast cancer had spread to my hip. The doctor was supposed to call, but he didn't. If I'd had a cell phone during that time, I would have hung it from my neck. In lieu of that, I stayed within earshot of the house phone, feeling like a dog inside an invisible security fence.

My daughter, who had worked as an office manager for a group of oncologists, suggested I call the orthopedic surgeon's office again. "Be nice," she said. "Don't take out your anger on the office workers. This isn't their fault."

I followed her advice and was talking to the doctor by the next day. He had been trying to contact me at the wrong number. And I had a stress fracture, not more cancer.

I pass on that advice when I hear others fret about delays in getting test results. I explain how office workers get so many reports back each day that they can hardly be expected to remember yours. Besides, it's the doctor's job to explain those results. Verify a number where you can be contacted, and thank them for their help.

A little kindness goes a long way. In time, some office workers and other health-care providers can become your much-needed friends. I am especially grateful for two women at my local oncologist's office. They recognize my voice on the phone, sincerely inquire how I'm doing, and ask how they can help me. Then, whether it's a prescription renewal, setting up a procedure, or asking the doctor for information — they act on it quickly and efficiently. You can't thank such people enough.

I'm also grateful for a claims manager who helps me with insurance. I almost went AWOL in a paper war when I was classified as a bone-marrow recipient for one type of cancer, and then developed another. Everyone was passing off payment, but the overdue notices kept coming my way. There wasn't a ceasefire till Mary took charge. This woman pursued my case with relentless skill until every bill was paid. When I sent her a note of thanks, she wrote back that I was on her list of people that she prays for every day: "Family, friends, and my claimants, too!"

Cancer introduces you to people you never expected to meet. Some of them become friends for life.

> *Pleasant words are a honeycomb,*
> *sweet to the soul and healing to the bones.*
>
> PROVERBS 16:24

We can't do what God has called us to do without involving others.

DARREL LE BARRON

CANCER IS SO LIMITED

It cannot silence courage

THE YEARLY CHECKUP

*F*ear is still only an inch deep," Ellie said about her husband's yearly checkups, years after he had been cleared of lymphoma: She'd wait in knots by the phone all morning until her husband Howard called, giving the official "all clear." Later, they'd both fall into each other's arms in tears, exhausted by the ordeal.

The problem with some types of cancer is that you can feel terrific and still have the disease. Other times, you may have symptoms, like a persistent cough, or pain in your belly, or fatigue — and yet have nothing more than "toe cancer." There's no such thing, of course, which is precisely the point. Eventually the symptoms go away, making you feel a bit silly about mentioning the problem to anyone, much less alerting the doctor, who orders tests that show nothing and just waste a lot of money.

Still, that yearly checkup is a challenge. It's a reminder, for one thing, of what you'd just as soon forget — a trying encounter with a deadly enemy that almost took your life. Like a war-weary veteran, you'd just as soon stuff those memories into a box and donate them to Goodwill.

This annual appointment is also a reality check, forcing you to wonder for the umpteenth time: *How safe am I, really, from recurrence?* I once saw a Canadian news documentary about breast cancer cells hiding out in tissue, just waiting for a trigger to activate them. How can we ever feel safe, once we've had cancer? How can we stop worrying?

One courage builder is realizing that for every checkup, with surprise results, you've had many years of routine, "everything is fine" ones. Thus abnormal results are the anomaly, not the norm.

Another courage builder is choosing to view a yearly checkup as another milestone. God has brought us safely through cancer another year and will continue to carry us into the future — regardless of what the doctor may find. We can mark this as a time to thank God for healing, to renew our commitment to trust him no matter what, and to celebrate one more year on the way to glory.

PARTICIPATING IN TREATMENT

We have choices," my doctor said at my last checkup. He couldn't have said anything sweeter. After slogging through nine months of treatment for leukemia, I couldn't do it anymore. I was so depressed that I no longer wanted to live. Like Elijah, I prayed, "I have had enough, Lord. Take my life." My world had shrunk to all-or-nothing thinking. I could either do chemo and die emotionally, or not do it and die physically. Neither was particularly acceptable.

The word *choices* took the bars off that kind of thinking. It blew the roof off my self-imposed prison. As the doctor sorted through the options — discontinue treatment altogether; take only one of three drugs; try something different — I felt hope stirring. I was no longer a passive recipient of a medical protocol; a blank tablet on which others would scribble prescriptions; a lump of flesh to be infused. I was actually a walking, talking, participating human being.

Why are choices so important? For one thing, they put the skids on a disease that has sent you thundering down the track like a runaway train. There are no stop signs, no yield signs, no beware-of-curves signs on this trip. It's just full speed ahead with you hanging on by your fingernails.

Choices move you from the back of the train to the front. If you're not in the driver's seat, at least you have the full attention of the conductor. You feel less at the mercy of others; more in control of what happens to you.

Choices also affirm you as a participant in your treatment. If you have no say in what happens to you, resentment and anger can build inside. Rather than expressing those feelings, you turn them against yourself — or against others who try to help you.

But the true empowerment of choices is knowing you can hand them over to God, trusting that he is in control of your life and will guide you and your doctor to make the right decisions. That gives you courage to participate — and rejoice — in treatment.

LIVING WITH RECURRENCE

For sixteen months I had been free of lymphoma. Rituxan, the magic bullet of non-Hodgkin's treatment, had targeted the malignant cells in my groin, chest, and abdomen, obliterating them as well as accompanying symptoms such as night sweats, itching, and fatigue. I felt terrific — until the morning I was chatting with someone at work and happened to rub the skin above my left collarbone.

More lumps.

The doctor had warned me about recurrence, saying I shouldn't get my hopes up about being cured. Still, hope, optimism, denial — whatever, kept me from looking in that direction. I felt great, therefore, I was.

When CT-scans and blood work confirmed that the lymphoma was back, I had to shift my thinking about cancer. Instead of regarding it as an opponent that needed to be dealt a one-time, knock-out punch, I had to think of it as a persistent annoyance that would have to be dealt with periodically for the rest of my life. Instead of cure, I had to think chronic disease.

In a way, that kind of thinking gives you courage to move on. Sure, you get weary of fighting this seemingly endless battle. You get tired of driving to the hospital, sticking your arm out for blood draws, waiting for bags of drugs to drip into your veins, picking up prescriptions to minimize side effects. But you get through it by the grace of God, the prayers of his people, your stubborn will to beat this thing out of your life, and the promising advances of medicine.

The apostle Paul had a chronic disease. We don't know exactly what it was — headaches, epilepsy, eye problems — but he pleaded with the Lord at least three times to take away this "messenger of Satan." God didn't do that. Instead Paul had to learn to live with the condition, trusting that God knew what was best for him. In the apostle's weakness, he learned to lean on God's strength. What's more, God's power was made evident to others through Paul's chronic illness.

Every day we live gives us courage to take on another day. And to prove to others that God's way is best.

TRYING NEW THINGS

*C*ancer can improve the quality of your life. It can give you the courage to break out of old patterns and try something new.

Some of that courage comes from realizing what it means to know that our days are numbered; that the end point of our life has slipped out of the fog, achieved definition, and is now moving toward us. And because we sense the finish line, we want to do everything we possibly can until the race is finished. So we take on challenges that we've put off for years, like starting a support group, reconciling with a sister, or even cleaning out the basement. We begin to live a kind of now-or-never approach to life.

Some of that courage comes from having faced fear. We've confronted the biggest bully of our life — cancer — and survived, and that gives us the courage to face up to other intimidators. So, whatever it is that's paralyzed us into inactivity before — fear of failing, fear of taking a risk, fear of loss, fear of what people might say — now looks trivial. We begin to sort through things we wish we had done and reconsider them outside the lens of fear.

I know one cancer survivor who sold her house, bought an RV, and began traveling the country, reconnecting with people. I know another who stopped saying "I wished I could 'a" and started taking piano lessons; another who stopped making excuses and began writing a book; another in an abusive relationship who finally got some counseling and began standing up for herself.

But on another level, courage to try new things comes via an experience that so shatters your life that you can't help but come back together a new way. Cancer brings you to the end of yourself, realizing you can do nothing to save yourself. You lean heavily on God because he is all you have.

And, as Psalm 40 says, he picks you up, puts your feet on a rock, and gives you a firm place to stand. He puts a new song in your mouth and a hymn of praise on your lips so that "many will see and fear and put their trust in the LORD" (Psalm 40:3). He gives you courage to try new things.

The LORD will guide you always,
he will satisfy your needs in a sun-scorched land
and will strengthen your frame.
You will be like a well-watered garden,
like a spring whose waters never fail.

ISAIAH 58:11

Consider it pure joy . . . whenever you face trials of many kinds,
because you know that the testing of your faith develops perseverance.

JAMES 1:2

We all die. Not living is the failure.

SIDNEY J. WINAWER, M.D.

CANCER IS SO LIMITED

It cannot invade the soul

SOUL RECOGNITION

D ad lay dying in the family room. I hadn't seen him for six weeks, so Mom warned me: "He can't see you — he's blind. But he'll know you."

She was right. Though Dad's body had wasted away from the tumor that bloated his belly, though he looked more like he was ninety instead of sixty-one, though his eyesight had failed because of malnutrition, he still knew me.

"Hi, Phyl," he said. "Did you have a good trip?"

He couldn't see me, and I could hardly recognize him, but we still knew each other. We could communicate soul to soul.

What is our soul, anyway? Certainly it's not what's most visible to others. I've had long hair, short hair, curly hair, and none, but my hair doesn't really define me. I've been a babysitter, bank teller, waitress, and editor, but that doesn't reveal my soul, either. What I look like, what I do, what I've accomplished — these things are a part of me, but they don't define who I really am.

My family knows more of me than most other people. They've seen me shuck bravado along with my work clothes and slump, defeated, into the nearest chair. They've walked with me out of a doctor's appointment, knowing I've turned to ice, and the melt-down will soon begin.

They're so attuned to my feelings that they can sense them by phone. "Are you okay?" my husband will ask from somewhere in Minnesota. "Do you want me to come home? How about dinner out tomorrow night?"

Still, do they really know my soul? If they did, would they be repulsed by how I vacillate between compassion and spite, tenderness and being judgmental? Would they back away from the deep dark hole in me where depression, fear, and anger swirl?

Would they be shocked by what tempts me to sin, what makes me cower like a child?

Sometimes I'm blind even to my own soul. But God isn't. As Hagar, the handmaiden of Sarai, said in the desert, "You are the God who sees me" (Genesis 16:13). And he is not repulsed. Rather, he picks me up, carries me in his arms, and assures me of his saving love.

Cancer can invade my body. It can swell it, waste it, cripple it, and blind it. But, it cannot invade my soul — for it is safe with God.

> *Let him who walks in the dark,*
> *who has no light,*
> *trust in the name of the LORD*
> *and rely on his God.*
>
> **ISAIAH 50:10**

Show me, O LORD, my life's end
and the number of my days;
let me know how fleeting is my life.
You have made my days a mere handbreadth;
the span of my years is as nothing before you.
Each man's life is but a breath.

PSALM 39:4 – 5

The people walking in darkness
have seen a great light;
on those living in the land of the shadow of death
a light has dawned.

ISAIAH 9:2

Other refuge have I none;
Hangs my helpless soul on Thee;
Leave, ah! Leave me not alone,
Still support and comfort me.

CHARLES WESLEY

THE WILL TO LIVE

My youngest sister, Barb, had given up. Several years ago, her oldest child, Joey, had been diagnosed with a malignant brain tumor. He was still alive after surgery and radiation, but he would struggle the rest of his life with brain damage. Now, the year-old baby, Corinna, had a brain tumor eerily similar to her oldest brother's. The growth was so huge that it took up a third of her brain cavity.

As Barb waited while surgery was performed on the baby, she couldn't even hope that this time things would be different. "Don't put Corinna through what Joey went through," she pleaded with God. "Just take her."

Finally, the surgery was over. As Barb walked over to the bed where her baby lay, she dreaded what she would find. As she took Corinna's hand, however, the baby opened her eyes and said, "Mama!"

Barb wept, knowing she and her husband would do everything it took to honor their daughter's will to keep going.

The will to live is an integral part of the human spirit. It's part of our DNA, our core, our soul. Our lives are short, to be sure; some of us won't live to age seventy, or, "if by strength," age eighty (Psalm 90:10). In between we may experience such pain and sorrow, the psalmist says, that "we finish our years with a moan" (Psalm 90:9).

Yet everything in us wants to hold on to life. We come out of cancer surgery minus a breast or kidney or several feet of intestine and are told we'll need months of radiation and/or chemotherapy that will burn our skin, erode our strength, and make our hair fall out, and we say, "Bring it on. I want to live!"

We have known suffering and pain and loss, to be sure, but we have also known the goodness of life: the delicate sky paintings of sunrise, the soft warmth of an awakening child, the sweetness of a tree-ripened peach, the aching loveliness of marital union.

More than that, we have felt the compelling love of the One who made us, and saved us from the dark sin within us, and now challenges us to live a new way for him. And because of that, life is really worth the living.

Because of the LORD's great love we are not consumed,
for his compassions never fail.
They are new every morning;
great is your faithfulness.

LAMENTATIONS 3:22 – 23

My comfort in my suffering is this:
Your promise preserves my life.

PSALM 119:50

I have learned never to underestimate the capacity of the human mind and body to regenerate — even when the prospects seem most wretched.

NORMAN COUSINS

TRUSTING LIKE A CHILD

Teresa said her grandma was 83, but she didn't think of herself as old.

"Does she look in the mirror and wonder who that old lady is?" I quipped.

"Yes, but she doesn't *feel* old," Teresa said.

"Maybe that's because inside we still feel like children?" I asked.

"Exactly. The soul doesn't age."

We who've lived awhile know how age affects the body. As time goes by, we collect wrinkles around our lips, dark spots on our arms, bruises under our eyes, and bumps on our feet. On a perfectly nice walk, our knees give way. Our hips ache from resting too long in bed. Everything fleshy sags or jiggles.

Cancer takes its toll, too. Though outwardly we appear much the same, what's underneath our clothing tells a different tale. Wide, white scars indent the breast, the back, the belly. A slight bulge in the chest whispers of the insertion of a portable catheter. Mottled skin reflects a reaction to a chemo drug. Some of us who have lost a breast or part of a limb and have been reconstructed have learned to sit, lie down, and walk differently. We buy egg-crate liners for our mattresses to sleep better at night, slide hymnals behind our backs during church, and remind ourselves not to twist our torsos by crossing our legs.

Our souls, by contrast, remain relatively childlike. Even though outwardly we look mature and in control, inwardly we still react like we have never grown up. We still smart like a kid at a public reprimand, still sting when someone passes us up for someone else, still hope for something wildly wonderful when unwrapping a gift or opening the mailbox. Like little kids, we're still tempted to eat what we shouldn't, spend what we don't have, and try to weasel our way out of the consequences of our wrongdoing. We still lie, cheat, steal, covet, and break all of God's commandments, even after a lifetime of asking forgiveness for sin and committing our lives to Christ.

Thankfully, we're still capable of childlike trust, as well. Though our bodies are frail and beaten down, our souls still cling like newborns to the promise of salvation through the blood of Jesus Christ. Time after time we stumble in our brokenness to the Savior, begging to be made whole again.

And — wonder of wonders — the Master does not turn us away. Rather, he gathers us into his arms and assures us, "Let the little children come to me, and do not hinder them, for the kingdom of heaven belongs to such as these" (Matthew 19:14).

> *Surely God is my salvation;*
> *I will trust and not be afraid.*
> *The LORD, the LORD, is my strength and my song;*
> *he has become my salvation.*
> *With joy you will draw water*
> *from the wells of salvation.*
>
> ISAIAH 12:2 – 3

SOUL FOOD

I'm a foodie. After finishing one meal, I look forward to the next. In between, I like opening my drawer at work or the fridge, searching for something salty, crispy, cool, or sweet.

Part of my obsession with food derives from my attempts to control it. I was chubby as a child, which no doubt pleased my mom, who equates a good appetite with health. I began questioning my weight as a teen, when I saw that my best friend, Margene, was attracting more boys that I. Was it because she was two sizes smaller? Still, I didn't do much about my weight until I was in college and was babysitting for a neighbor, who lost nearly a hundred pounds through TOPS (Take Off Pounds Sensibly). I began asking questions. Over the next six months I began counting calories, altered my eating, and lost twenty-five pounds. Boys who had been just buddies were suddenly asking me out.

Over the years since, I've kept my weight in check, but not without effort. I've counted calories, kept food diaries, cut back on fat, learned to like artificial sweeteners, and started exercising. I've tried nearly every diet imaginable, from the sensible to the insane.

The greatest irony of having cancer has been its impact on my weight. I've lost dozens of pounds to surgery, to chemotherapy, and to stress. There have been times when pants were so loose I needed belts to hold them up; when dresses were so baggy I needed to cover them with jackets or sweaters. I'd look at my naked body and wonder, "Where did it go?"

It went of course, along with my appetite; I was too weak or nauseous or tired to think about food, much less lift it to my mouth. And, finally, released from this "god of the stomach" (see Philippians 3:19), I had more time to feast on heavenly things. I devoured books of the Bible, devotionals, and sermons, and filled up to bursting with CDs of my favorite hymns and oratorios.

As my body wasted, my spirit put on pounds.

I'm healthy today and back to weight watching — but with
a difference. Each time I'm tempted to obsess about a little extra
padding, I give thanks for health and an appetite for what really
counts: soul food.

> *Praise the LORD, O my soul,*
> *and forget not all his benefits —*
> *who forgives all your sins*
> *and heals all your diseases,*
> *who redeems your life from the pit*
> *and crowns you with love and compassion,*
> *who satisfies your desires with good things.*
>
> PSALM 103:2 – 5

The joy of surmounting obstacles which once seemed unremov-
able, and pushing the frontier of accomplishments further —
what joy is there like unto it?

HELEN KELLER

CANCER IS SO LIMITED

It cannot steal eternal life

DARKS AND LIGHTS

The "I Spy" quilt I made for my grandson included thirteen shelves on which 166 bottles were arranged, each containing something different: candies, animals, bugs, toys, cartoon characters, kids. Some bright figures were against a dark background, while other characters were surrounded by white. The trick was positioning the bottles so that they didn't disappear into each other but stood out in a pattern of darks and lights.

Our lives are a bit like quilts. For the most part, our days are filled with good things: love in marriage, raising children, moving from place to place, finding jobs, making friends. We progress from one year to the next, giving thanks for how God has blessed us.

But between the bright times are dark patches; jobs we've lost, projects we've messed up, work we've left undone, blowups we've had with our kids, nagging concerns about money, and of course, struggles with diseases such as cancer.

Perhaps our good times would not be so meaningful without the bad ones. We don't know how refreshing a full night of uninterrupted sleep can be until we've suffered nights of insomnia. We don't relish a walk around the block until we've been too weak to get out of bed. And we are never so grateful for health as when we hear that our cancer is in remission.

But contrasting siuations aren't the only answer. Ecclesiastes 3:11 tells us, "[God] has made everything beautiful in its time." All of life's uprooting and tearing down and weeping and suffering can become beautiful in its own time — but it is difficult to see that until we're looking back on it. Then we get an inkling of how God has drawn us to himself through those hard times, making us "mature and complete, not lacking anything" (James 1:4).

In the meantime, we keep going, trusting that one day we will pass beyond this place of contrasts to a place where everything shimmers in true color in the light of our Eternal King.

BEYOND THE PAIN

Sometimes what gets me through a difficult medical procedure is thinking beyond it. When two technicians were digging for a vein to thread a tube from my arm to my heart, I projected myself ahead to when my sister and I would get back to clowning around. "We'll turn on a movie, or order lunch, or walk to the gift shop," I told myself.

That technique helped me make it through the last mile of a 25-K race: Instead of concentrating on my heaving chest and my dragging feet and the last long incline, I'd think of the long table full of orange slices and popsicles just ahead, the big hugs from family and friends, the long soak in a hot bath.

That technique also helped me through painful times in relationships. When the hurt of being betrayed and rejected by someone I loved and trusted so twisted my insides that I could barely function, I would tell myself, "We'll get through this. We'll work through this and make it to the other side."

This technique is hardly original with me. It's the essence of what people of faith have been practicing from the beginning of time. Like us, Jesus walked this earth, experiencing its joys and its sorrows. He had loving parents, though at times they failed to understand his calling. He had companions who traveled with him everywhere, listening to his teachings, yet, when their Master was in intense pain, his friends stayed away. Jesus' miraculous works of healing attracted great crowds; but the same people turned on him when he was sentenced to death on a trumped-up charge. Always, Jesus kept going by fixing his eyes on his Father, trusting him for what would come next.

In the midst of pain and suffering, do what Jesus did: think beyond it to eternity.

God will redeem my life from the grave;
he will surely take me to himself.

PSALM 49:15

LASTING MOMENTS

There are some moments I wish would last forever.

- Picking blueberries in the dew of early morning, listening to the birds, feeling the sun's warmth, and trading thoughts with my daughter as our pails fill.
- Sitting on lawn chairs in a park with my husband, picnicking on cheese and bread and olives, then settling back to watch "Hamlet."
- Snapping photos of the grandkids scampering on the beach as the sun sets fire to the sky behind them, then finally sinks into the water.

In a sense, those moments do last forever — at least in memory. And recalled, they still make me smile or sigh. They also make me long for more.

Likewise, we've experienced moments with God here in life that are so precious that we yearn for more to life. I still remember the morning

I realized that I could no longer go on living. "I can't do it any-more. Take me — all of me," I prayed.

After that, life changed. I no longer felt obligated to be with God; I *wanted* that time. Without daily contact with him, I felt shorted, uneasy, restless. The more I got of the Lord, the more I wanted.

I remember how I felt going into surgery for breast cancer as well; how I held onto God's promises for dear life as I was wheeled into a world of stainless steel and bright lights and people in masks. Though my fingers and toes were like ice, my heart was at rest, fearing no evil even in this valley of the shadow of death, because God was with me. I could have dwelled in that peace forever.

God was with me, too, a year ago, when I was hospitalized for leukemia. I awoke one night, feeling dark and cold and afraid. "If I die tonight, am I ready?" I asked myself. Doubt crowded me like black angels picking off the covers of my faith. "Only through the blood of Christ," I whispered back. I repeated that, childlike, till the blackness receded.

Cancer can steal some of our moments; it can make us sick, uneasy, and afraid. But it cannot steal precious moments with God — or the assurance that one day we will step out of our broken-down bodies and walk with him, fully healed, on the shores of eternity.

When I am afraid,
I will trust in you.
In God, whose word I praise,
in God I trust; I will not be afraid.

PSALM 56:3 – 4

Jesus said, "I give them eternal life, and they shall never perish;
no one can snatch them out of my hand.
My Father, who has given them to me, is greater than all."

JOHN 10:28 – 29

Faith in God, who knows every fiber of our being and loves us in spite of our sins, is the narrow gate which connects this world with the next.

HENRI J. M. NOUWEN

A Place for Us

My husband, Paul, and I had time to kill before my room in the hospital was ready. So we ate lunch, wandered through the gift shop, flipped through magazines, watched people — and tried not to harass the clerk at the desk about when we could go upstairs.

When we finally got to my room on the fifteenth floor, we realized, in part, what had taken so long. The dark cherry shelving was polished, the bed crisp with fresh linens, the washroom stacked with supplies. There was no trace of the former occupant; this was my space. No one could see me without washing hands and pulling on gloves, masks, and gowns. I was in a sealed ward that no one could enter without first passing through a space that locked off outside air. Those inside this ward had to be protected from germs.

My room was beautiful; it overlooked the city of Chicago. By day I watched people and traffic scurry far below me. By night I watched the lights brighten the tall buildings surrounding me. Of all the hospitals I knew, this was by far the most luxurious.

I felt safe, protected, well-cared for in that room. It became a kind of Bethel for me, a place where I felt very close to the gate of heaven, and where I promised to continue my journey as long as God would be with me.

After nearly a month, I went home. That's when I realized how small and cramped that little room had been. The sky, which I could only glimpse through a window, was suddenly vibrant around me. People and cars moved past me, life-size. The world was so full of color, beauty, movement, and energy that I could hardly take it in.

I realized what a place of trial that little room had been. In it I had experienced all the predicted side effects of chemotherapy:

nausea, vomiting, rashes, bleeding, hair loss, fevers, pressure headaches, infection in the fluid around my heart and brain. Now that I was home, I realized how sick I had been.

In some ways, that little room is like this world. It is all we know of home. But even now, Jesus is preparing a place for us in heaven. It's a place we don't know much about yet, but we can trust that it will be good. Jesus himself will take us there. And we will look back on this time on earth, this vale of suffering, as something we merely passed through on our way to something better.

For God so loved the world that he gave his one and only Son,
that whoever believes in him shall not perish but have eternal life.

JOHN 3:16

Even though I walk
through the valley of the shadow of death,
I will fear no evil,
for you are with me.

PSALM 23:4

Jesus said, "If I go and prepare a place for you, I will come back and take you to be with me that you also may be where I am."

JOHN 14:3

Our destiny is home with our Father in heaven. It is so easy on this journey to lose sight of our destination and to focus on the detours of this life instead. This life is only the trip to get home.

BOB SNYDER

One hour of eternity, one moment with the Lord, will make us utterly forget a lifetime of desolations.

BOB SNYDER

In the arms of God, there is no time. There is only love. That's what we call eternity, not endless time, but endless love. If you have love, you have all the time in the world — right now.

JOHN ROBERT MCFARLAND

CANCER IS SO LIMITED

It cannot conquer the spirit

BACKUP PRAYER

For weeks I had been praying for God's direction about my chemotherapy. After a six-week break from three drugs that had all but killed my will to go on living, much less my ability to fight cancer, I had agreed to begin one of the drugs again.

ATRA knocked me off my feet. I spent three days in bed with a killer headache caused by fluid buildup around the brain. I took a breather, then tried a reduced dose of the drug. More headaches — plus insomnia, depression, and fatigue. I walked into the doctor's office, feeling like a failure. I had flunked this chemo — what was next? Arsenic?

But my doc had something up the sleeve of his white coat. After listening to my litany of woe, he gave me the news. "Preliminary reports on new studies strongly suggest that people in molecular remission from APL (my type of leukemia) who went through maintenance therapy did not do significantly better than those without," he said. "I'm taking you off chemo." I felt like life had been handed back to me.

Sometimes when we pray, we don't know what to pray for. We try asking questions, then we speculate how God might answer. Then we ask more questions with those answers in mind. But the process seems wrong. So finally we give up trying to guess and just beg God to tell us what to do. We feel so weak and so directionless and so helpless that we can hardly pray.

Here, then, is the miracle. Romans 8:26 tells us that when we are in such a state, "the Spirit himself intercedes for us with groans that words cannot express." The Spirit prays for God's will for us when we don't have a clue what that is. And the Spirit "who searches our hearts" (v. 27) negotiates answers for us that far surpass anything we might have dreamed up on our own.

Can cancer kill our spirits? Not if it rests, even at its weakest, in the Spirit of God. For, as Paul says in verse 37: "In all these things we are more than conquerors through him who loved us."

BLAMELESS

Some of us don't need friends like Job's to beat up on us — we beat up on ourselves. When we get cancer, we wonder if it's because of something we did. Was it the water we drank? The smoking we did in college? Not enough exercise? Poor diet?

We can dig at ourselves spiritually, too. Is God punishing us for some secret sin? Is he trying to loosen our grip on things to make us more dependent on him? Is he trying to get at our spirits by humbling our bodies?

Such questions may be worth pondering — for a while. But we shouldn't get stuck in them. As my friend Donna says, "Life's too short." Cancer can prompt us to make changes in our lives, one of which should be learning to take better care of ourselves.

We could try listening to our bodies, for example, tuning in to its complaints. For example, if we have a perpetually sore shoulder, we may be sitting incorrectly, or tensing too long at the computer. A few stretching exercises could help. If we nod off mid-morning, maybe it's because we skipped breakfast. We might need a pick-up snack, like some yogurt or a granola bar.

We should take note of the times we feel especially good, too. Are we energized after a weekend of banking sleep to cover the shortages of the week, at the finish of a great bike ride, after a long walk? Maybe we should take more time for such body builders.

We also need time to tend our spirits. The Bible tells us that our bodies are God's temples (1 Corinthians 3:16). Imagine that — these faltering, scarred, broken down, diseased bodies — receptacles of the Spirit of God!

What's more, we have been washed, sanctified, and justified in the name of the Lord Jesus Christ and by the Spirit of God. That means we no longer have to lug around a load of regrets or beat ourselves up spiritually because we have cancer. We are blameless in the sight of God. As 1 Corinthians 6:19 – 20 says, "You are not your own; you were bought at a price. Therefore honor God with your body."

Restore us, O LORD God Almighty;
make your face shine upon us,
that we may be saved.

PSALM 80:19

If the Son sets you free, you will be free indeed.

JOHN 8:36

God demonstrates his own love for us in this:
While we were still sinners, Christ died for us.

ROMANS 5:8

Every night I turn worries over to God. He's going to be up all night anyway.

MARY C. CROWLEY

RACE FOR THE CURE

The first time I went to a breast-cancer support group, I came home so exhilarated that it took me hours to settle down. I don't remember who the guest speaker was that night; what wowed me were nearly a hundred women laughing, chatting, and hugging each other — and all of us had cancer. Life hadn't ended for them; it had just taken an unexpected turn. And they were riding it well.

Ostensibly missing from that group, however, were dozens of women who had attended the group for several years, then moved on. Many of those long-term survivors never had breast cancer again. They had raced for the cure and won.

We who have cancer are most encouraged by people who have beaten cancer. My friend Diane, who has recurrent ovarian cancer, was discouraged by statistics indicating how many women die of the disease. What lifted her spirits was reading about women who were living ten years or more after first being diagnosed.

Likewise, the most helpful cards I received were from women whose struggles with cancer had long receded into the past. They were so beyond cancer that they rarely talked about it. But some took the time to send me a note with scribbled bits of their history. And that helped me believe that I, too, could be cured.

We with cancer hope for a cure. We ask God for grace to get through what we must — chemotherapy, radiation, countless tests, doctor visits — in order to leave the whole wretched experience of cancer behind us.

Not all of us will be cured, but all of us will find healing in one way or another. Because of cancer, some of us will trade in old goals for new ones. Some of us will clear out time and space so we can relax a bit and enjoy life. Some of us will dump toxic relationships and find new, more supportive ones. Some of us will discover the arms and lips and hearts of family in ways we've never known them before.

And some of us — hopefully all of us — will find the truth of God's promise in a new way: "'For I know the plans I have for you,'" declares the LORD, "'plans to prosper you and not to harm you, plans to give you hope and a future'" (Jeremiah 29:11).

Our bodies may fade and falter, but in that hope, our spirits will be renewed until the day when every part of us races across the final finish line to the Ultimate Cure.

> *Let us throw off everything that hinders*
> *and the sin that so easily entangles, and let us run with*
> *perseverance the race marked out for us.*
>
> HEBREWS 12:1

The life you clutch, hoard, guard, and play safe with is in the end a life worth little to anybody, including yourself, and only a life given away for love's sake is a life worth living.

FREDERICK BUECHNER

VICTORY NO MATTER WHAT

I was already hooked up to my I.V. when the chemo nurse stopped by and asked if she could seat a young girl next to me who was receiving her last treatment for breast cancer. "You remember what that was like," the nurse said. "Will you talk with her?"

I knew what she was referring to. You'd think that by the last day of chemo, a person with cancer would be celebrating. Indeed, the nurses often make a party out of it, bringing in cake, flowers, and a "graduation" certificate. But despite all of the hoopla, there's an underlying current of anxiety about discontinuing drugs that are killing cancer in your body. What will happen now that you've stopped? How will you know if the cancer has come back? Who will be watching you to make sure that doesn't happen? One of my breast cancer buddies kept a stash of her leftover chemo pills. When she felt anxious about ending treatment, she'd pop a pill. I remember feeling vulnerable, too. If the wait between doctor visits was too long, I'd start worrying about symptoms: was that node in my neck growing? Was the mole on my leg getting darker? What about the morning cough — should I have it checked out? The fear of recurrence after treatment ends messes with your mind; it erodes your confidence and drags on your spirit.

Over time, I have come to learn the wisdom of my mother's advice: The longer you survive, the safer you'll feel. Even though I have had various types of cancer and several recurrences over the years, I have learned to stop anticipating cancer and to enjoy the stretches between, realizing the truth of Scripture: "Do not worry about tomorrow, for tomorrow will worry about itself" (Matthew 6:34).

If we truly believe in God, Romans 8:15 tells us, we are given a spirit that does not become a slave to fear. Rather, we are given the "Spirit of sonship," assuring us that no matter what happens, we are God's children forever. In the end, this promise gives us victory over cancer — no matter what!

Sources

Anderson, Greg. *Fifty Essential Things to Do When the Doctor Says It's Cancer*. Penguin Books: New York, 1993.

Armstrong, Lance, with Sally Jenkins. *It's Not about the Bike*. Berkley Books: New York, 2001.

Barnes, M. Craig. *Hustling God*. Zondervan: Grand Rapids, MI., 1999.

Bence, Evelyn, compiler. *Mornings with Henri J.M Nouwen*. Servant Publications: Cincinnati, OH, 1997.

Benjamin, Harold H., with Richard Trubo. *From Victim to Victor*. Dell Publishing: New York, 1987.

Buechner, Frederick. *Wishful Thinking: A Theological ABC*. Harper and Row: New York, 1973.

Carmody, John. *Cancer and Faith*. Twenty-Third Publications: Mystic, CT, 1994.

Cobble, Nancy, M.D., with Joy Sawyer. *Holding Heaven and Earth in One Hand*. Judson Press: Valley Forge, PA, 1998.

Cousins, Norman. *Anatomy of an Illness*. W.W. Norton and Co.: New York, 1979.

Cowman, Mrs. Chas. E. *Streams in the Desert*. Cowman Publications: California, 1950.

Freeman, Rusty. *Journey into Day*. Judson Press: Valley Forge, PA, 2000.

Greene, Bob, and D.G. Fulford. *Notes on the Kitchen Table*. Doubleday: New York, 1998.

Groopman, Jerome. *The Anatomy of Hope*. Random House: New York, 2004.

Gulley, Philip. *Front Porch Tales*. Multnomah Books: Sisters, OR, 1997.

Hymns for the Living Church. Hope Publishing Company: Carol Stream, IL, 1978.

Keller, Helen. *The Open Door*. Doubleday & Co.: New York, 1957.

Kelly, Bob. *Worth Repeating*. Kregel Publications: Grand Rapids, MI, 2003.

Lovett, Sean-Patrick, editor. *The Best Gift Is Love: Meditations by Mother Teresa*. Servant Publications: Cincinnati, OH, 1982.

McFarland, John Robert. *Now That I Have Cancer I Am Whole*. Andrews and McMeel: Kansas City, MO, 1993.

Merton, Thomas. *No Man Is an Island*. Dell: New York, 1962.

Nessim, Susan & Judith Ellis. *Cancerville: The Challenge of Life After Cancer*. Houghton Mifflin Company: Boston, MA, 1991.

Porter, Margit Esser. *Hope Is Contagious*. Simon and Schuster: New York, 1997.

Siegel, Bernie S., M.D. *Love, Medicine, and Miracles*. HarperCollins: New York, 1986.

Slung, Michele. *Momilies: As My Mother Used to Say...* Ballantine Books: New York, 1985.

Spurgeon, Charles. *Morning and Evening*. Zondervan: Grand Rapids, MI, 1965.

The Belgic Confession, Article 13

The Heidelberg Catechism, Question and Answer 1 of Lord's Day 1

The Shorter Catechism, Question 98

Ten Boom, Corrie. *The Hiding Place*. Baker Book House: Grand Rapids, MI, 1971, 1984.

Ten Boom, Corrie. *Tramp for the Lord*. Fleming H. Revell Company: New York, 1978.

Tengbom, Mildred. *Why Waste Your Illness?* Augsburg Publishing House: Minneapolis, MN, 1984.

Vanauken, Sheldon. *A Severe Mercy*. Bantam Books: New York, 1979.

Van Dyke, Henry. *The Upward Path*. Harold Shaw Publishers: Carol Stream, IL, 1995.

Water, Mark, compiler. *The New Encyclopedia of Christian Quotations*. Baker Books: Grand Rapids, MI, 2000.

Weir, Al B., M.D. *When Your Doctor Has Bad News*, Zondervan: Grand Rapids, MI, 2003.

Winawer, Sidney J. *Healing Lessons*. Little, Brown and Company: New York, 1998.

Wright, H. Norman. *Winning over Your Emotions*. Harvest House Publishers: Eugene, OR, 1998.

Yancey, Philip. *Finding God in Unexpected Places*. Moorings: New York, 1995.

At Inspirio, we'd love to hear
your stories and your feedback.
Please send your comments to us
by way of email at
icares@zondervan.com
or to the address below:

inspirio

Attn: Inspirio Cares
5300 Patterson Avenue SE
Grand Rapids, MI 49530
If you would like further information
about Inspirio and the products we create,
please visit us at:
www.inspiriogifts.com
Thank you and God bless!